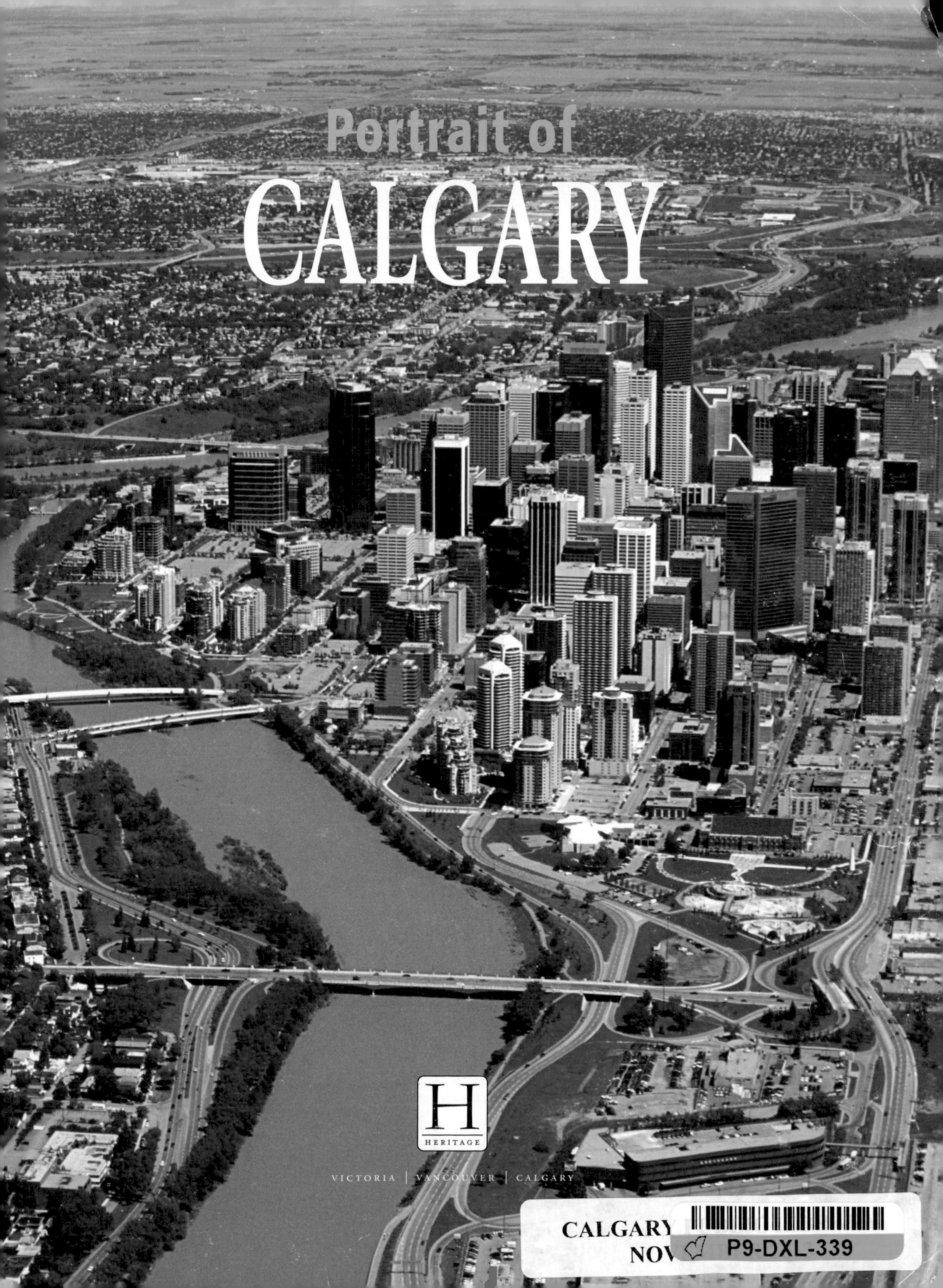
Portrait of
CALGARY
H
HERITAGE
VICTORIA | VANCOUVER | CALGARY

Heritage House Publishing Company Ltd.
heritagehouse.ca

LIBRARY AND ARCHIVES CANADA CATALOGUING IN PUBLICATION
Bradley, Andrew, 1962–
Portrait of Calgary / Andrew Peter Bradley.

ISBN 978-1-927051-36-8

1. Calgary (Alta.)—Pictorial works. I. Title.

FC3697.37.B72 2013 971.23'38040222 C2013-900024-0

Edited by Kate Scallion
Proofread by Lara Kordic
Cover design by Jacqui Thomas

Cover photos: A view of downtown Calgary that includes the Bow Building, the Calgary Tower and the Centre Street Bridge (front); a cowboy prepares to leave the pen before a wild ride, red barn in a canola field (back) by Andrew Bradley
Title page: Calgary's towering downtown is a sharp contrast to the sprawling suburbs and vast prairies.
Copyright page photo: Pedestrians crowd Eighth Avenue (more popularly known as Stephen Avenue Mall) on a lovely summer day.

This book was produced using FSC®-certified, acid-free paper, processed chlorine free and printed with vegetable-based inks.

Heritage House acknowledges the financial support for its publishing program from the Government of Canada through the Canada Book Fund (CBF), Canada Council for the Arts and the province of British Columbia through the British Columbia Arts Council and the Book Publishing Tax Credit.

Canadian Heritage Patrimoine canadien
Canada Council for the Arts Conseil des Arts du Canada
British Columbia Arts Council

17 16 15 14 13 1 2 3 4 5

Printed in Canada

CALGARY

top A transport truck cruises north along the open highway.

WELCOME TO CALGARY

opposite The ski jumps at Canada Olympic Park rise in the distance over colourful summer wildflowers.

top The bowed roof of the Saddledome is unlike any of the skyscrapers that shape the rest of Calgary's skyline.

One hundred and twenty-five years ago, you could be forgiven for not recognizing the name Calgary. Hardly more than an outpost, the site located at the fork of the Bow River and Elbow Creek was only known to a handful of pioneers and prospectors who passed through the area in search of rich pasture lands or fortunes promised in the goldfields of Yukon and Alaska.

The beginnings of modern-day Calgary stretch back to 1875 when the North West Mounted Police were ordered to build a fort there to protect the western Canadian fur trade from American whisky traders. Within a few decades, Calgary was already transforming into the city we know today.

Nearly 100 years before the first European, John Glenn, settled in Calgary, David Thompson was the first European on record to visit what we now know as Calgary. Prior to colonial settlement, the area was considered Blackfoot territory. Peigan bands were known to have camped along the Bow River during the winter months, and First Nations presence in the area has been traced back at least 11,000 years.

In the 1880s, Calgary was already an agricultural and industrial centre. The Canadian Pacific Railway reached the area in 1883, a year before Calgary was officially incorporated as a town. By 1894, the town was big enough to be declared "The City of Calgary."

top Spanning the Bow River, the Peace Bridge is a pedestrian footbridge that was completed in 2010.

The population of Calgary grew rapidly up until the Second World War. Agriculture and ranching were the mainstays of the city. Although oil was discovered in Alberta in 1902, the oil boom didn't being until 1947 when the province's massive reserves were discovered and subsequently tapped. Calgary quickly became Canada's commercial and industrial centre for the oil and gas industry and has maintained that position ever since.

Although Calgary might have a reputation as an oil boom town, there's much more to the city than that. Its rich ranching and western heritage is celebrated every year during the Calgary Stampede. Tourists flock to the city year round, chasing both summer and winter adventures. There are countless festivals celebrating the city's arts and culture.

The 1988 Winter Olympic Games focused the world's attention on Calgary as it hosted 57 nations. A rich sporting legacy grew out of these games and the city is home to world-class athletes in several sports. The Olympic Oval at the University of Calgary boasts the top speed skaters in Canada—and the world—and the ski jumps and bobsled track have been training grounds for several generations of Canadian Olympians. And all these athletic accomplishments don't even include the Calgary Flames or the Calgary Stampeders, Calgary's national hockey and football teams, which help feed Calgary's ceaseless appetite for action-packed sports, or any of the other great athletic venues in the city.

top Built for the 1988 Winter Olympic Games, the Olympic Plaza buzzes with activity on summer days.

right A team of skilled dancers perform the Chinese dragon dance.

Geographically, Calgary is bordered by grassland and foothills. It is perfectly situated to be the "Gateway to the Rockies." A beautiful drive west along the TransCanada Highway takes you to Canmore, Banff, Lake Louise, Jasper and beyond—world-renowned destinations in their own right. To the south and east of Calgary, attractions like Waterton Lakes National Park, Head-Smashed-In Buffalo Jump, Drumheller, Dinosaur National Park and the Badlands are all within a few hours' drive.

So dig in; come and see what the heart of the Canadian west has to offer.

opposite Bright lights and busy streets make it seem like Calgary never slows down.

top Skaters crowd Bowness Park. In the summer, it's just as popular for picnickers.

right One of Calgary's rapid transit trains waits at a station.

CALGARY'S HEART AND SOUL

opposite The Calgary Tower stretches up almost forever from this angle.

top Red tulips and new leaves frame Calgary's municipal building.

Take a stroll through Calgary's downtown core and you will find the beating heart of a strong and vibrant city. The towering skyscrapers and construction cranes are proof that this city continues to grow and flourish.

Even to the casual observer, Calgary seems to have found that delicate balance of living history and modern technology. The Inglewood shopping district along Ninth Avenue is actually Calgary's oldest neighbourhood, going back all the way to 1875. It was established adjacent to Fort Calgary and has the honour of being "Calgary's original main street." Today Inglewood is known for being one of the most diverse and eclectic areas of town, with dozens of locally owned shops and restaurants.

A 10- to 15-minute walk from Inglewood brings you to downtown Calgary. You're only limited by your imagination when it comes to finding things to do and see with literally thousands of shops, business, restaurants, cafes, galleries and more to choose from.

All around you can find examples of Calgary's unique blend of old and new. From the Calgary Philharmonic Orchestra to the foot stompin' country music of the western bars, the old-world charms of the Stephen Avenue Mall facades to the glass and steel structures that continue to push Calgary's magnificent skyline ever higher.

Typical of the old and new blend is Calgary's City Hall. Built in 1911 and a designated National Historic Site of Canada, its sandstone walls stand tall and proud against the striking architecture of triangles and mirrored glass that is the Municipal Building.

Presiding over the heart of Calgary is one of the most recognizable landmarks: the

Calgary Tower. Rising 160 metres from the streets below, the Tower's rotating restaurant provides a culinary experience high on anyone's list of to-dos and, in true Calgary fashion, treats visitors to sweeping vistas that leave them in no doubt as to where they've been, where they are and where they are going. Even though taller buildings such as the 58-storey Bow Building stretch well above the Calgary tower's 190-metre antenna, it is still easy to distinguish the Calgary Tower's unique shape on the city's skyline.

Many of Calgary's downtown buildings are linked by the +15 Skywalk—the largest elevated pedestrian walkway in the world. Comprising more than 60 bridges and covering more than 18 kilometres, the +15 Skywalk connects more than 100 downtown office buildings. The climate-controlled walkways make it easy and comfortable to get around the city regardless of the weather outside.

As in the architecture, Calgary's spirit can be seen in the massive wall murals and streetside sculptures of stone and bronze that pay tribute to the past and present achievements and reflect future aspirations. Going on a self-guided art tour of downtown Calgary will introduce you to many of Calgary's cultural treasures. The public art celebrates the history and heritage of the city as well as showcasing talented contemporary artists.

Even if you only spend a day downtown, by the end of it you will have discovered more than just Calgary's strong heart; you will have witnessed the spirited soul of a city steeped in the tradition of the west and boldly moving towards the future.

top The ceiling of the Chinese Cultural Centre is an intricate and beautiful mosaic.

opposite The tallest building in Calgary, the 58-storey Bow Building was completed in 2012.

JUGO

opposite Kensington, a popular Calgary neighbourhood, looks like a charming winter wonderland with a dusting of snow illuminating the street.

top Many of Calgary's downtown buildings feature murals that depict the city's history. This mural, *Legacy*, is on the back of the Petroleum Club.

right The Alberta Children's Hospital's colourful exterior is just one feature that makes this building unique. It opened in 2006.

top The lions on the Centre Street Bridge in Calgary make it the most identifiable bridge in the city. Built in 1916, it is also one of Calgary's oldest bridges. These lions are replicas of the original lions and were installed in 2001 when the bridge underwent a major restoration.

left One of Calgary's +15 Skywalk bridges illuminated for night use.

opposite The sandstone walls of City Hall rise majestically, even though several buildings nearby are much taller than this lovely old building.

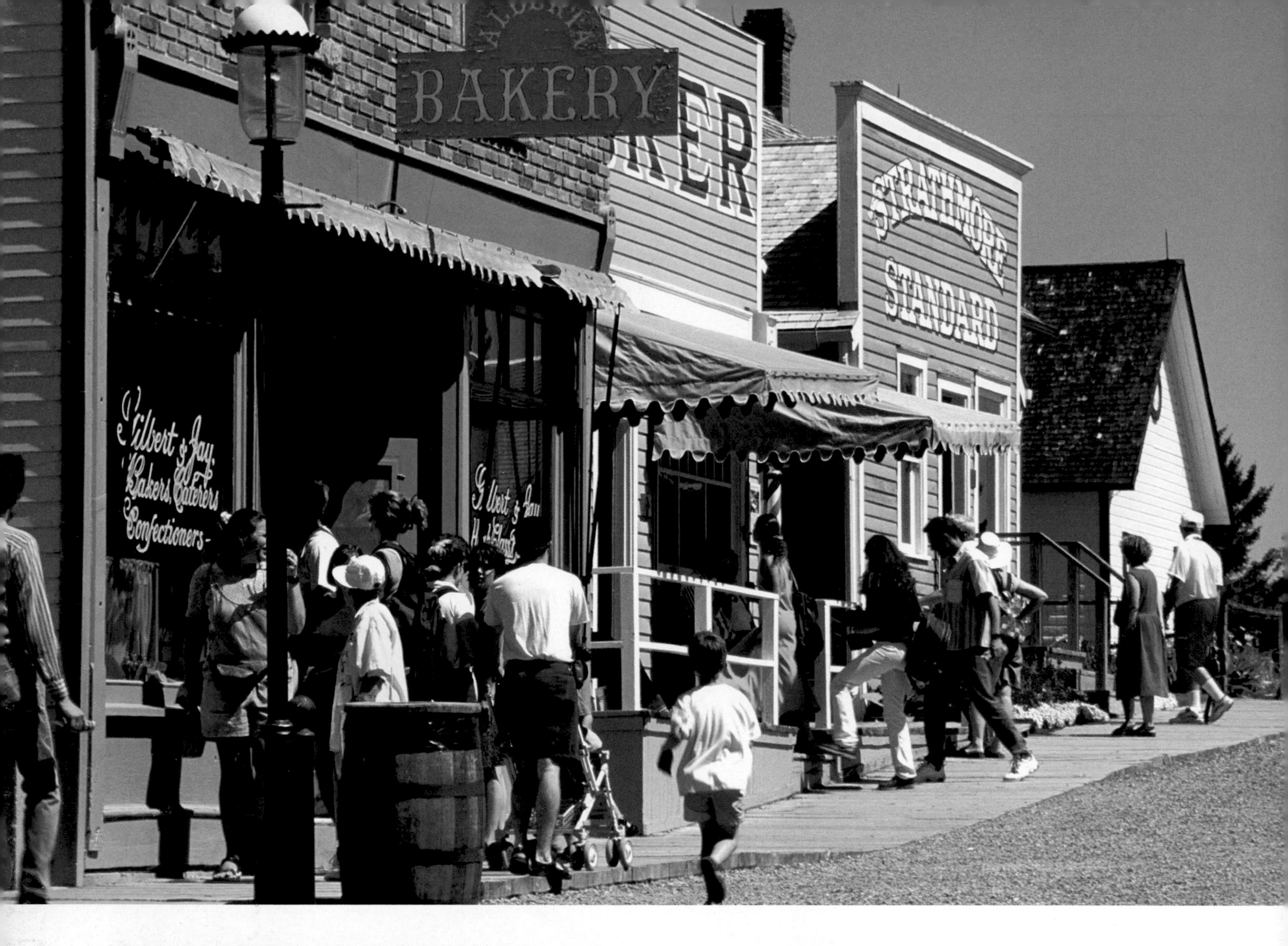

top The "main street" of Calgary's Heritage Park is crowded with tourists on a glorious summer day.

left *The Famous Five* sculpture commemorates the five women who sought to have women legally considered as "persons" so they could be appointed to the Senate. A sculpture identical to this one is found on Parliament Hill in Ottawa.

opposite The *Family of Man* sculpture is located outside the Calgary Board of Education offices. Originally part of the British Pavilion at Expo '67, the statutes were purchased by Maxwell Cummings and Sons and donated to the Calgary Board of Education. Each figure is nearly 6.5 metres tall.

GETTING OUT AND ABOUT

opposite A cyclist cruises along one of Calgary's many bike paths.

top Fifth Avenue Place is just one of Calgary's hundreds of skyscrapers.

If you judge a city by its green space, Calgary is sure to please. The City of Calgary maintains more than 700 kilometres of bike paths and 7,800 hectares of parklands. There are more than 5,300 designated park sites in and around the city. One of the biggest parks within the city limits is Nose Hill Park. Located in the northwest quadrant of the city, it covers more than 11 square kilometres, making it one of the largest urban parks in North America and home to a healthy wildlife population. The oldest park in Calgary is Central Memorial Park. Land for the park was donated in 1899 and the park was completed and opened in 1912. It has undergone redevelopment a few times since its opening day, including a substantial rehabilitation from 2009 to 2010. Calgary's Remembrance Day ceremonies are held in this park each year. The Calgary Olympic Plaza is another downtown gem. It was built as the medal presentation site for the 1988 Winter Olympic Games and now is a popular spot for festivities and events year round. In the winter, it is home to a refrigerated outdoor skating area.

Calgary also has several immaculately maintained gardens, including the Beaulieu Gardens at Lougheed House. Other notable gardens are the Century Gardens and the Devonian Gardens. The Century Gardens are also in the heart of downtown and are a popular place for nearby office workers to picnic on their lunch breaks. The Devonian

top Some of the displays at Fort Calgary show more recent times, like this re-creation of Maple Leaf Station circa 1913.

Gardens are actually a downtown indoor oasis, perfect for a hit of summer greenery if the weather outside is dreary.

The Calgary Zoo is another wonderful outdoor attraction. It's readily accessible by Calgary's light rail transit system. You'll know you're at the right stop to get off when you see giant dinosaurs peeking over the fence by the train. Although the zoo started off small in 1929, it now has several extensive exhibits, including features on South America, Africa, Eurasia, Australia, the Arctic and Antarctic as well as a Canadian Wild Exhibit. The Zoo also has a prehistoric park that includes life-size dinosaur installations recreated in the same geographical environment that would have existed millions of years ago.

If inside attractions and history are more to your liking, there are plenty of places to check out. Heritage Park Historical Village is one of Canada's largest living history museums. Its four sections represent four different time periods in Calgary's history. Heritage Park is probably Calgary's best example of the living past. With Calgarians dressed in period costumes, visitors can actually take part in the day-to-day goings on of a typical old-fashioned prairie town made up of Calgary's real historic buildings. Similar to Heritage Park, Fort Calgary is another great living history museum that invites you to come visit the place where Calgary began. It is due for a multi-million-dollar makeover that includes constructing a new building.

top The Glenmore Reservoir is used to supply Calgary with water, but it is also a popular recreational destination.

The Glenbow Museum, located near the Calgary Tower, has more than 20 different galleries and features extensive holdings on cultural history, ethnology, military history and mineralogy. With more than 1 million objects in its collection, it would be hard not to spend hours at the Glenbow. The Calgary Military Museums is another attraction well worth visiting for a day. Other Calgary museums include the Aero Space Museum, the Grain Academy and Museum, and Lougheed House. Calgary is also home to several galleries, including Art Central, the Museum of Contemporary Art Calgary and, of course, the Art Gallery of Calgary.

Another fantastic Calgary attraction is its new science centre, the Telus World of Science, or the Spark. Calgary's first science centre, originally called the Calgary Centennial Planetarium, opened in 1967. In 1987, the Planetarium was transformed into the Calgary Science Centre after a four-year bid to bring a science centre to Calgary. In 2011, the Spark replaced the original Science Centre, opening in a new specially designed location and featuring countless interactive exhibits.

top The McDougall School is a lovely sandstone building that was completed in 1908. It was Calgary's first normal school, the schools where teachers were trained. It was also the government offices for former Alberta premier Ralph Klein.

left The Olympic Arch acts as a welcome gate to the University of Calgary.

opposite This Tyrannosaurus Rex is just one of many life-size dinosaurs at the Calgary Zoo.

top From a distance, the scope and size of the Spark is much easier to discern. If it is this big from the outside, just imagine how many fun displays there are inside.

left The Calgary Zoo is home to many primates, including this gorilla.

right The Military Museums in Calgary have displays featuring life-size re-creations of military life from several different eras, including the First and Second World Wars.

top Fall colours light up the trees in Nose Hill Park.

left The "downtown campus" building was renovated to LEED silver standards for the University of Calgary.

top The atrium at the Calgary Military Museums features the mural *Honour Welcome*, which was installed in 2006. Each of the mural's 240 panels has an accompanying story.

right The McEwan Student Centre is a cheerful, open space where students can relax at the University of Calgary.

A CITY OF CHAMPIONS

opposite A Calgary Flames hockey mask seems to peer down at the Calgary Tower from its perch on the side of the Saddledome.

top An equestrian clears the formidable Canada Flag jump.

In February of 1988, Calgary was brought to the forefront of international attention as the proud host of the Olympic Winter Games. The success of the games brought tremendous global recognition and a renewed sense of pride to the city, and left a legacy of world-class sporting facilities that have since changed the face of Calgary.

One of Calgary's most iconic landmarks, the Scotiabank Saddledome, is one of these great facilities. It first opened its doors in 1983 and was the Olympic hockey and figure skating venue. Today it is the home of the Calgary Flames. The Saddledome is situated on the legendary Stampede grounds, and when it's not packed to the rafters for hockey games, it is used for rodeo events, lacrosse, figure skating, curling, concerts and other major public events. In fact, the Western Hockey League's Calgary Hitmen call the Saddledome home, as do the Calgary Roughnecks, the city's National Lacrosse League team.

Nowhere else is the competitive spirit of the winter Olympics more alive than at the University of Calgary's Olympic Oval. With an impressive seating capacity and meticulously maintained ice surface, the Oval continues to see champions made and records broken. It has proven its claim many, many times to be "the fastest ice in the world."

Built to accommodate such Olympic events as the ski jump, downhill slalom, bobsled and luge, the slopes of Canada Olympic Park's $72-million facilities are shared by visitors,

top Just beyond downtown, the Saddledome is home to the Calgary Flames, but it is also used for concerts and minor league hockey.

locals and aspiring medallists alike. At the bottom of the slopes, an interpretive centre pays tribute to the success of the winter games, while the 90-metre ski jump provides visitors with city views to the east and Rocky Mountain vistas to the west. Canada Olympic Park now includes summer facilities that accommodate mountain biking, as well as an ice house that lets visitors take a run on a short indoor luge track. This outstanding venue is continually updated, keeping its facilities in top-notch shape so that the City of Calgary will continue to produce great athletes. In 2008, Canada Olympic Park was declared the new home of Canada's Sports Hall of Fame. Construction of a new facility at the park to house the Hall of Fame began in 2008, and the doors officially opened in 2011.

Not all of Calgary's sporting facilities, nor its recreational pursuits, are Olympic by nature. While the Saddledome is Calgary's premier hockey arena, McMahon Stadium, for example, is to football what the Saddledome is to hockey. The proud flagship for Calgary's many football fans, McMahon Stadium is home to the Calgary Stampeders. Likewise, the recently updated Max Bell Arena is a regular venue for Calgary's minor hockey leagues.

The Talisman Centre is undoubtedly the largest and most diverse training facility in the city. Built in 1983 for the Western Canada Games, the cavernous interior of the Talisman Centre's semi-rigid structure contains an Olympic-size pool complete with 10-metre diving platform, 200-metre indoor running track, multiple gyms, squash, tennis

top A rider and his horse gracefully clear a jump at Spruce Meadows.

right Speed skaters zip around the Olympic Oval, training for their next race.

and basketball courts, and even a rock climbing wall. The facility has undergone several multi-million renovations and facelifts over the past decade, maintaining its status as one of Calgary's premiere athletic facilities.

To the south of Calgary, the combined talents of man and mount are brought together in a different type of competition that has made the exceptional facilities of Spruce Meadows highly regarded in equestrian circles.

From flags to facilities, the Olympic spirit is still very much alive in Calgary, continuing its success as a city of champions.

top The Calgary Flames play in front of a packed house at the Saddledome.

left Skeleton and bobsledding are two events that athletes can practise on Canada Olympic Park's bobsled track.

top The Winsport Markin MacPhail Centre is an incredible athletic facility for winter sports.

right Curling is a quintessential Canadian winter sport and is popular with people of all ages.

opposite Flags from every nation that participated in the 1988 Olympics still proudly wave in the wind at Canada Olympic Park.

top The roof of the Talisman Centre is a "semi-rigid" structure, which allows lots of natural light to filter through.

right The Calgary Stampeders face off against the Saskatchewan Roughriders at McMahon Stadium.

top The ski jumps at Canada Olympic Park are one of the city's most visible reminders of the 1988 Olympics.

left Snowboarding has become a very popular winter activity at Canada Olympic Park, although the sport was barely even invented when Calgary hosted the Olympics.

opposite The Talisman Centre has some of the best aquatic facilities in Calgary.

STAMPEDE CITY

opposite Fireworks light up the sky over the Stampede grounds.

top Cowboys wait for their turn in the rodeo ring.

Mention Calgary to anyone and you will be hard pressed not to mention the Calgary Stampede in the same breath. The roots of the Stampede date back almost as far as the city itself. In 1886, an agricultural fair was held to promote Calgary, hoping to entice eastern farmers and ranchers to move west. The first Calgary Stampede was hosted in 1912, the brainchild of American promoter Guy Weadick. It took until 1923 for Stampede became an annual event. In fact, the 1923 Stampede probably bears the closest resemblance to what the Stampede looks like today; traditions such as pancake breakfasts and chuck-wagon racing first appeared that year.

More than 1,000 events take place during the 10-day rodeo. From the opening parade to concerts and barbecues, it's impossible to resist the fun of the Stampede. The whole city becomes part of the action. Calgary's business core takes on a distinctively western flavour; offices and shop fronts are decorated in true western fashion, with hay bales and wagon wheels while Calgarians carry on business dressed in full western garb.

A virtual Mecca for country enthusiasts, the Stampede brings together some to the world's finest cowboys in what is widely regarded as the world's richest rodeo—more than $1 million is up for grabs as prize money. Competitors come from all over North America and as far away as Australia and Brazil. The competition is fast and furious for the incredible

purse offered in each of the five major events, including bull riding, barrel racing, steer wrestling and bronc riding. The controversial chuckwagon races are one of the Stampede's most exciting daily events, not to mention hotly contested and inherently dangerous. While the rodeo is the Stampede's biggest attraction, there are countless other events to keep you entertained, including concerts and fair rides.

top This cowboy keeps his seat despite the wild bucking of his horse.

First Nations culture and history have been a part of the Stampede since its inception. Although Stampede organizers had to fight for their inclusion in the first Stampedes, now there is a Native village set up that offers arts and crafts and re-enacts traditional elements of Native lifestyles. This has become one the Stampede's biggest attractions. The five official tribes that represent the Indian Village at the Stampede are the Tsuu T'ina, Piikani, Stoney, Kainai and Siksika Nations.

More than 100 years later, the Calgary Stampede is still hosted on the same grounds. Substantially increased, upgraded, renovated and improved, the Stampede grounds are more than 193 acres in size. They have become a year-round hub for Calgarians, home to a casino, retail businesses and the Scotiabank Saddledome.

Anyone who has survived the 10 action-packed days of country and western festivities will understand why the Calgary Stampede is known as "The Greatest Outdoor Show on Earth."

top There are plenty of fair rides at the Stampede for those willing to risk their lunches.

Even when the Stampede is not in town, it's easy to see Calgary's strong ties with its cowboy beginnings. The western spirit is evident everywhere from downtown to the cowboy way of life found in the surrounding prairies. It is alive and well in the real-life cowboys who still make a living from the area's ranching and farming businesses and communities. Alberta beef, for example, is big business indeed, and one of the area's most successful exports. Throughout the region's foothills and prairielands, modern-day cowboys can still be seen on horseback, driving cattle or just surveying the land. Calgary's satellite towns of Airdrie, Strathmore, Okotoks and Cochrane celebrate the area's western heritage annually with their own rodeos and particular brand of festivities.

From the rolling prairies to the downtown skyscrapers, the spirit of the west is alive and strong in the hearts and souls of the people who find their place here in the heart of the Canadian west.

top The bright lights of all the rides can have a dizzying effect.

left A cowgirl speeds through a rodeo event at the Stampede.

opposite A grass dancer takes part in the Stampede festivities.

top The Stampede parade entices people dressed in outrageous costumes to take to the streets.

left A rodeo clown waits for some action.

top First Nations from around Calgary participate in the Stampede parade. The five official tribes that represent the Indian Village at the Stampede are the Tsuu T'ina, Piikani, Stoney, Kainai and Siksika Nations.

right A cowboy wrestles a steer in the dirt.

top First Nations drummers draw a crowd at the Stampede.

left Horses are crowded into a holding pen prior to a rodeo event.

opposite Taking a spin on a Ferris wheel is a great way to get a good view of all the action.

top The RCMP show off their equestrian skills as part of some Stampede demonstrations.

left Marching bands are just one of the many musical elements in the Stampede parade.

top A cowboy prepares to leave the pen before a wild ride.

right There is a full range of music, concerts and shows to provide evening entertainment during the Stampede.

top Although controversial and dangerous, chuckwagon races are very popular events at the Stampede.

left Massive tents are set up all over Calgary during the Stampede, housing events such as pancake breakfasts.

opposite Spinning hoops are just part of this man's traditional dance.

OIL AND AGRICULTURE

opposite The dusky prairie sky gives this industrial site an idyllic glow.

top A combine harvests the rich bounty found in the farmland outside of Calgary.

Approximately 65 million years ago, the southern Alberta area was a vast inland sea alive with prehistoric marine life. Through time, the seas gave way to swamp and eventually to a lush green landscape dominated by tall fertile forest and perhaps some to the worlds largest living land animals to ever walk the face of the earth.

Down through the ages, the dinosaurs too were to succumb to the marches of time, leaving a legacy of fossil remains, well preserved in such fine institutions as the Royal Tyrrell Museum located to the east of Calgary. But the greatest fossil legacy of all was the vast oil and gas resources, which fuel Calgary's booming economy and contribute to prosperous secondary economies such as building and construction as more and more people flock to Calgary.

Natural gas was first discovered near Alderson, Alberta, in 1883. Oil was discovered in Alberta in 1902, but the oil boom didn't begin until 1947 with the success of the Leduc oil well. From 1947 onward, Calgary's population and economy grew by leaps and bounds as it became the corporate and administrative centre for oil and petroleum companies in Canada. Alberta produces nearly 70 percent of Canada's crude oil and has some of the largest crude oil reserves in the world. The city is home to the National Energy Board and the Natural Gas Exchange, and the Alberta Crown owns 97 percent of the oil sands mineral rights.

top A red barn is just a speck on the horizon of this canola field.

The ever present pumpjacks and oil derricks scattered about the landscape are a constant reminder of the "Oil Capital's" commitment to oil exploration. But recessions in the past decades have helped curb Calgary's dependence on the oil and gas industry to fuel the city's economy.

Agriculture has always been a mainstay of the economy in Alberta. Not only do the prairies yield a rich wealth of oil, but they also provide the farming industry with a fertile basis for the region's other equally important export crops.

Beef is Alberta's primary agriculture export; there are more than 3 million head of cattle farmed in the province, and the worldwide market continues to hunger for prime Alberta beef.

The main grain crops are wheat and canola. Distinctive yellow canola fields are easy to pick out from the sky or highway as you make your way into Calgary. Rolling fields of wheat and other grains border the highways from every direction, and there are still a few grain elevators casting long shadows across the prairies, reminiscent of Calgary's traditional economic mainstay and the farming legacy that continues to thrive today.

top Rig workers prepare a lease for drilling operations.

right The action of a pumpjack is not unlike a cowboy on a bucking bronco.

GATEWAY TO THE ROCKIES AND BEYOND

opposite Bighorn sheep are just as common on the road as they are on mountain and cliff sides.

top A rural road rolls through the foothills on the way to the mountains.

Calgary not only has hundreds of great attractions, but it is also within a few hours' drive of several other amazing destinations, with the Rocky Mountains to the West and the Badlands to the south.

No one could ever come to Calgary without experiencing the sheer magnificence of the Canadian Rocky Mountains. A mere hour's drive west along the TransCanada Highway, the mountain parks attract millions of visitors each year. Heading west, Kananaskis Country (or K-Country) is impossible to avoid as it covers more than 4,000 square kilometres, right up to the outskirts of Canmore. It is home to several large provincial parks and some of the best skiing and mountain biking that Alberta has to offer, not to mention golf and pretty much anything else an outdoors person could want all year round.

Just past K-Country's western border lie Canmore and Banff. Canmore has come a long way from its coal-mining past. Its charming main street features all sorts of shops. The Canmore Nordic Centre Provincial Park is open year round for mountain biking and cross-country skiing. In fact, the Canadian national cross-country ski team calls Canmore home.

Fewer than 30 kilometres down the highway from Canmore is Banff National Park. A revered destination for decades, Banff is home to world-famous hot springs and is a

top A hiker pauses along a ridge.

popular place in every season. From wildlife watching to hiking, camping and skiing, or luxurious spas and shopping, Banff has something for everyone.

Each year migratory patterns bring hundreds of elk to graze on the lush grasslands surrounding Banff. It's not unusual to find the park's most prevalent wildlife strolling around the streets or finding a free lunch in someone's flowerbed. Bighorn sheep are also very popular throughout the park. A small herd of bighorns found along the Lake Minnewanka loop road will bring any visitor as close to the local wildlife as someone would ever want to get. Being somewhat more elusive, the occasional grizzly, black bear or moose can be seen along the park's highways and byways.

Of course, the area's greatest attraction is its stunning scenery and pristine wilderness. Winding through the Rockies, the TransCanada Highway and Icefields Parkway present even the most casual travellers with breathtaking views of snow-capped mountains, glaciers and valley vistas.

Winter months bring much-welcomed snow to the mountains. Several world-class ski resorts throughout the Rockies attract skiers and snowboarders from all over. With snowfalls that continue well into spring, the slopes of Sunshine and Lake Louise have been known to provide exceptionally long ski seasons. From Banff, it is only a short drive to Lake Louise, another spectacular national park. A few more hours along the road bring

top Canoes lie along a dock at picture-perfect Lake Louise. People can rent canoes and enjoy paddling on the lake in the summer.

right The Johnston Canyon Falls in Banff National Park, not far from Castle Mountain Junction.

you to the Icefields Parkway, which goes by the Columbia Icefields up to Jasper.

Heading south or east from Calgary, you'll encounter remarkably different geography from the towering Rockies. The rolling foothills flatten out into vast plains with river valleys snaking through. The badlands near Drumheller or Dinosaur Provincial Park feature some of the most bizarre geography in Canada, with hoodoo spires and strange plateaus being the prominent features on the horizon, majestic in their own unique way. The beautiful landscape around Calgary is part and parcel of the beautiful landscape throughout Alberta, and Calgarians are lucky to have such diversity within a few hours of their special city.

top Herds of bighorn sheep nimbly scramble around cliffs as if there's no chance of falling or danger.

left A fox is not as camouflaged by the flowers as it thinks it is.

opposite Two Jack Lake is a short distance from downtown Banff, but you wouldn't know by its pristine beauty.

next The Fairmont Banff Springs Hotel was built by the Canadian Pacific Railway and opened in 1888.

Andrew Peter Bradley is an Australian-born photographer who left his home on the Gold Coast in 1990 to travel the world. After living in LA, New York, Toronto, Banff and Fort McMurray, he finally landed in Calgary and stayed there for 15 years. Enamoured with Calgary's western culture, dynamic architecture and the fabulous Rocky Mountains, Andrew has produced thousands of images that have been used in various publications to promote Calgary. He has produced two other books, *Portrait of Edmonton* and *Portrait of Alberta*. Andrew currently lives on Vancouver Island where he follows his other passion, sailing.